CHILDREN SUNDAY SCHOOL LESSONS: THE PARABLES AND TEACHINGS OF JESUS: VOLUME 1

Copyright 2012 by Stephen R. Wilson

Published 2012
Printed in the United States of America

ISBN: 978-1482023916

D1173220

Also Available from Rev. Stephen R. Wilson:

Youth Bible Lessons

Created: Youth Bible Studies on Genesis 1-11 and the Book of Job

Samuel the PROphet: Youth Bible Studies on 1 Samuel

King David, the Might Runt: Youth Bible Studies on David's Road to the Throne

Children Bible Lessons

Created: Children Sunday School Lessons for Genesis 1-11

Father Abraham: Children Sunday School Lessons on Genesis 12-50

Slaves to Conquerors: Children Sunday School Lessons on Exodus through Joshua

The Lord's Top Ten: Children Sunday School Lessons on the Ten Commandments

The Judges (and Ruth): Children Sunday School Lessons

Miracle Children: Christmas Sunday School Lessons

Jesus Starts His Work: Children Sunday School Lessons

Jesus Teaches on the Mountain: Sermon on the Mount
Children Sunday School Lessons

Children Sunday School Lessons: The Parables and
Teachings of Jesus: Volume 1

Children Sunday School Lessons: The Parables and
Teachings of Jesus: Volume 2

Children Sunday School Lessons: The Miracles of Jesus

He Came, He Saw, He Conquered: Children Sunday
School Lesson on the Death and Resurrection of Jesus

The Rock: Children Sunday School Lessons on the
Apostle Peter

Paul: The Odd Apostle - Children Sunday School
Lessons on the Apostle Paul

Followers of the Christ: Children Sunday School
Lessons from Acts and the Epistles

Non-Fiction

Last Days: A Biblical Guide to the End Times

Church History in Modern Language! The Letters of
Clement Paraphrased into Contemporary English

Fiction

The Gifted: Book 1: In the Beginning

The Gifted: Book 2: Coming of Age

The Gifted: Book 3: Heavens and Earth

Lesson 1: Counting the Cost

Needed: Bibles, Legos or building blocks of some sort

Lesson: (Note: Always allow students enough time to think about and to give their answers to the questions before clarifying the teaching.)

(Have students take turns reading Luke 14:25-26, or read it yourself.)

Jesus said that if we want to be His disciple, or His follower, then we have to hate our parents and our family. But does Jesus really want us to hate our parents and our families? (No.)

Jesus wants us to love our parents and our families, but He wants us to understand that we have to love Him more. Jesus is God so if we want to be Jesus' follower, we have to love Him more than anything, even more than our own parents. You even have to love Jesus more than you love yourself and your life. Jesus has to be the most important thing to you.

(Have students take turns reading Luke 14:27-33, or read it yourself.)

(Pass out nine building blocks to each student and tell them to build a tower that is ten blocks high using only their blocks. Don't tell them you're only giving them nine blocks.)

How many blocks do you have in your tower?

You only have nine blocks in your tower, but I told you to make a tower that was ten blocks high. Didn't you know you count your blocks first to know whether you had ten blocks to use or not?

Jesus said being a Christian is kind of like building a tower. When you build a tower, you have to make sure you have enough to be able to finish it so that it reaches all the way to the sky. And when you say you want to believe in Jesus and be His follower, you have to make sure that you're ready to believe in Jesus not just right now, but for your whole life, so that you can go to Heaven when you die.

Do you think you're ready to follow Jesus for your whole life?

(Pray with students to help them commit their lives to Christ.)

Lesson 2: What It Takes to be One of Jesus' Followers

Needed: Bibles, a large rock, optional camping supplies

Lesson: (Note: Always allow students enough time to think about and to give their answers to the questions before clarifying the teaching.)

Show camping supplies if you brought any. Ask students, How many of you have ever been camping? Did you like it?

What if you had to camp your whole life and not have a tent or a camper or anything? And you didn't have a house or an apartment to go live in? You just had to sleep on the ground and live outside all the time? And use a rock for your pillow (show rock)?

(Have students take turns reading Matthew 8:18-20, or read it yourself.)

Jesus said that He camped out most of the time. He said birds have nests to live in and foxes have holes in the ground that they can sleep in, but Jesus didn't have a house or even a pillow to sleep on. He usually had to sleep outside.

And He said that if we want to believe in Him, we have to be ready to do the same things He did. If Jesus asked us to, we would have to camp outside all the time. Whatever Jesus says, that's what we have to do.

Or maybe if someone wanted to arrest us because we believed in Jesus, we would have to run away and sleep outside. People in other countries are arrested if they believe in Jesus and sometimes they're even killed.

Believing in Jesus isn't easy. It's dangerous. And you have to think ahead of time, right now, if you're brave enough to believe in Jesus. Just like last week when we built that tower and had to think if we had enough bricks, you have to think if you're brave enough to believe in Jesus your whole life and can do what Jesus tells you to. You have to be brave enough to do whatever scary or not fun thing Jesus tells you to do. You have to be brave enough to be a Christian even if you get in trouble for it. You have to be brave. Who thinks they can be brave enough to follow Jesus? Who thinks they want to believe in Jesus their whole life?

(Have students take turns reading Matthew 8:21-22, or read it yourself.)

Another man asked Jesus to let him go bury his father and then he would come follow Jesus, but Jesus told him to let the dead bury their own dead and for him to follow Jesus. What did Jesus mean by saying that to the man? Did Jesus really not want the man to go to his father's funeral? (No.)

Jesus wants to love and take care of our families, but Jesus wants us to know that we can only be a follower of Jesus if we make Jesus the most important thing in our lives. Jesus has to be even more important to us than our own father, or our own mother, or our brothers or sisters or friends. Jesus has to be most important.

To be a follower of Jesus, you have to be brave and be able to do whatever hard thing Jesus tell you to do, and you have to make sure you love Jesus more than anything or anyone else in the whole world because Jesus is most important.

Lesson 3: The Calling of Matthew

Needed: Bibles

Lesson: (Note: Always allow students enough time to think about and to give their answers to the questions before clarifying the teaching.)

(Have a student read Matthew 9:9, or read it yourself.)

Matthew was doing his job, but when Jesus said, "Follow Me", Matthew got right up and followed Him. Why do you think Matthew didn't wait to follow Jesus until he got off work? (Matthew knew that nothing is as important as following Jesus. Jesus is the most important thing, no matter what we're doing.)

What was Matthew's job? (He was a tax collector.)

In those days, people hated tax collectors. The tax collectors' job was to take some of your money and give it to the king. But the tax collectors would always charge you too much money, more than the king said you had to give him, and then they would keep the extras for themselves. So most people probably didn't like Matthew because he stole from them and wasn't a very good person.

But then Jesus asked Matthew to follow Him and to believe in Him. Why do you think Jesus asked Matthew to follow Him when He knew that Matthew was stealing from people? (Jesus wanted to give Matthew a chance to change.)

(Have students take turns reading Matthew 9:10-11, or read it yourself.)

The Pharisees saw Jesus eating with tax collectors, those people who stole money, and all kinds of other bad people and they asked why Jesus was eating with them. They didn't think Matthew and his friends were good enough to hang out with Jesus because they did wrong things. They didn't think Matthew could change and be better. But Jesus knew that Matthew and his friends could change and be better.

Everyone stand up…Now everyone raise your hand. Raise it up as high as it will go…Is it up as high as you can make it?

Now everyone raise your hands a little more…It went up a little further, didn't it?

Jesus knows that we can always do more than we think we can and we can always do more than other people think we can.

People didn't think that Matthew could change and be better, but he did. He believed in Jesus and he stopped stealing and he became one of Jesus's twelve disciples. That was a very important job. And Matthew even got to write one of the books of the Bible. That's a really important job.

What I want you to think about today is that Jesus can change your life too. Even if you do bad things sometimes, like Matthew did when he stole from people, if you believe in Jesus, He will forgive you for those things and change you so that you don't do those bad things anymore. And He can use to do great and important things for Him, just like He used Matthew to do important things, like being one of His disciples or writing a book of the Bible.

Jesus can change you and make you be great for Him, no matter what other people think about you.

Lesson 4: Jesus, the Doctor for Our Souls

Needed: Bibles

Lesson: (Note: Always allow students enough time to think about and to give their answers to the questions before clarifying the teaching.)

Do you remember when we were talking about Matthew and Matthew's friends and about how some people thought that Matthew and his friends weren't good enough to be friends with Jesus?

Well, this is what Jesus told them.

(Have a student read Matthew 9:12, or read it yourself.)

"It is not the healthy people who need a doctor, but the sick."

Have you ever been to the doctor?

Why do people go to the doctor?

People go to the doctor when they're sick. They feel bad or they have a disease, or maybe they got hurt. Maybe they're even dying, and they have to go to the doctor to get better.

Well, did you know that just like our bodies get sick or get hurt, our souls or our spirits can get sick and get hurt too. Maybe it's because something bad or sad happened to us and it makes us feel bad on the inside, in our souls or our spirits. And the Bible says that we are all sick on the inside when we do bad things.

But Jesus said that He is the doctor for our spirits or souls. When we go to Jesus, He can help make us feel better from those bad and sad things that happen to us, and He can heal us from wanting to do bad things. Jesus is the doctor for our souls and we can go to Him whenever we feel bad on the inside.

What are some things that might happen to you to make you feel bad or sad on the inside, in your spirit or soul? (Someone dying, someone calling you a bad name, getting in trouble, doing bad things, etc.)

Jesus says that if we pray to Him, He is the doctor for our souls and He can make us feel better about those things.

The other reason people go to a doctor, though, is just to get a check-up. They don't feel bad. They just want to go in and make sure they're okay. Jesus also wants us to come to Him for a check-up every once in a while. Even if we're not feeling bad in our souls or spirits, Jesus wants us to get our spiritual check-up.

We can go to Jesus for our spiritual check-up by praying, going to church, talking about God with our parents or grandparents, and reading our Bible. We do those things just to make sure our souls or spirits are doing okay, just like we go to the doctor for our check-up to make sure we're doing okay.

So remember, we can go to Jesus when we feel bad on the inside and He's the doctor who can fix our spirits or souls. But Jesus also wants us to come to Him when we're not feeling bad so that we can get our spiritual check-up and make sure we're doing okay.

Lesson 5: Jesus the Groom

Needed: Bibles

Lesson: (Note: Always allow students enough time to think about and to give their answers to the questions before clarifying the teaching.)

How many of you have ever been to a wedding?

Are people happy when they get married or sad? (Happy.)

Everyone make a happy face.

(Have students take turns reading Matthew 9:14-15, or read it yourself.)

Jesus said that when He came down from Heaven when He was born, it was like He was getting married. That's because He loves us so much.

Everyone put your hands over your heart.

Jesus loves us even more than a husband and wife love each other.

But then Jesus died on the cross. How do you think Jesus' followers felt when He died? (Sad.)

Everyone make a sad face.

Why did Jesus die on the cross? (To forgive us for our sins so that we could be saved.)

But then, three days later, God raised Jesus from the dead and everyone was happy again.

Everyone make a happy face.

But then, forty days after that, it was time for Jesus to go back up to Heaven and everyone was sad because they couldn't see Jesus anymore.

Everyone make a sad face.

But Jesus said that someday, He will come back to Earth and will live with us forever. Then, we will all be happy…Everyone make a happy face…and we will never die or get sick or have anything bad happen to us ever again.

Lesson 6: New Wine into New Wineskins

Needed: Three large glasses, one small glass, tarps or towels

Lesson: (Note: Always allow students enough time to think about and to give their answers to the questions before clarifying the teaching.)

(Place tarps or towels around your demonstration area. Fill two of the large glasses with water. Pull out the small glass and say something like,)

We're going to pretend that this is you.

(Now pull out one of the large glasses filled with water and say,)

And we're going to pretend that this is all the great stuff Jesus wants to teach you.

(Pour the large glass of water into the small cup and let it overflow.)

What happened? Why did the water spill out?

Jesus said we can't learn everything He wants to teach us unless we change.

(Pull out the large empty glass.)

We have to change our lives. That means to stop doing the wrong things we do and start doing the right things. It means to believe in Jesus and give Him our lives. Then we will be able to learn all the great things Jesus wants to teach us.

(Pull out the second large glass of water and pour it into the empty large glass.)

If we want to learn everything Jesus wants to teach us, we have to be ready to change our lives.

Prayer: Everyone close your eyes. I want you to think for a second to yourself and ask Jesus if there's anything in your life He wants you to change…Ask Him if you're doing anything bad that He wants you to stop doing… Ask Him if there's anything good that He wants you to start doing.

Lesson 7: The Harvest is Plentiful

Needed: Bibles, Picture of a large ripe farm field

Lesson: (Note: Always allow students enough time to think about and to give their answers to the questions before clarifying the teaching.)

Have students take turns reading Matthew 9:35-38, or read it yourself.

Show students the picture of the farm field and ask, Do you see how big this farm field is? How many of you would like to go pick all these crops by yourself, without any help?

It would take a long time to do it all by yourself, wouldn't it?

What if you had some friends to help you? Would the work go faster then?

Jesus said picking crops is kind of like telling people about God. Jesus was walking around from town to town, telling people about God, but it was a lot of work to do that and He knew that He couldn't go to all the villages to tell everyone about God.

So Jesus told His disciples, "I want you to go tell people about God too. If you help Me tell people about God, then we can tell a lot more people than just Me doing it by Myself."

And that's what the disciples did. Just like Jesus, they went around in the villages and the cities telling people about God.

And that's what Jesus wants us to do too. He wants us to help Him tell people about God so that they can believe in God and go to Heaven with Him someday. So let's all help Jesus by telling everyone we know about God.

And remember, more people can learn about God when we're all helping to tell about Him.

Game: *Harvest Tag* – One person is It. They are "Jesus". When they tag someone, that person becomes a Disciple and helps "Jesus" tag others. Play until everyone has been tagged and has become a Disciple. The last person tagged is "Jesus" for the new round.

Prayer: Close your eyes and think of one person you would like to tag for Jesus, one person you would like to tell about God...Now say a prayer for that person...Now ask God to help you tell that person about God.

Lesson 8: Jesus Gives Everyone a Chance!

Needed: Bibles

Lesson: (Note: Always allow students enough time to think about and to give their answers to the questions before clarifying the teaching.)

(Have a student read Matthew 10:1, or read it yourself.)

What did Jesus give the twelve disciples power to do? (To make demons leave people and to heal sick people.)

Well, if Jesus gave the twelve disciples the power to do things like that, let's find out who the twelve disciples were.

(Have another student read Matthew 10:2, or read it yourself.)

Peter, Andrew, James, John. What were there jobs? Does anyone remember? (They were fishermen.)

Peter, Andrew, James, and John weren't rich, they didn't go to college. They just worked hard and went out on their boats and caught fish for people to eat.

 (Have another student read Matthew 10:3, or read it yourself.)

Thomas. Does anyone know anything about Thomas?

After Jesus died, Thomas didn't believe it when the rest of the disciples told him that Jesus had come back to life. He had to wait until he saw Jesus himself before he would believe it.

And what about Matthew? What does it say Matthew's job was? (He was a tax collector.)

And remember that people didn't like Matthew before he became a disciple because he used to charge people too much taxes and steal money from them.

(Have another student read Matthew 10:4, or read it yourself.)

Simon the Zealot. Someone who was a zealot was someone who wanted to fight and have a war against the Romans to make them leave Israel so that Israel could have its country back. He was a fighter.

Judas Iscariot. Does anyone remember the bad thing Judas Iscariot did? (He betrayed Jesus by telling the priests where Jesus was so that they could arrest Him.)

So some of the disciples were just regular people and some of them were even bad people. But Jesus made them all His disciples. He gave all of them a chance to follow Him. That's because Jesus loves everyone and He gives everyone in the world, no matter who they are or what bad things they've done, a chance to follow Him.

And it says that Jesus gave them power to drive out demons and heal people who were sick. The disciples were just regular people, but Jesus gave them power to do awesome, not regular things. The disciples weren't special by themselves. None of them had really good jobs or were rich or anything like that. But Jesus made them special when He made them His disciples and gave them power.

Jesus can make us special too. If we follow Jesus, then we're special because we believe in God and Jesus and Jesus will give us power.

What kind of power do you think Jesus will give you?

Jesus might not give you the power to heal sick people or to do other miracles like that, but He does give all of us power. He gives us the Holy Spirit to live inside of us and the Holy Spirit gives us the power to do the right things instead of listening to the devil and doing wrong things, and to tell people about Jesus.

Those are the best powers of all, because when we do the right things and when we tell other people about Jesus, then that makes God happy with us.

Lesson 9: Don't Be Afraid of People

Needed: Bibles

Lesson: (Note: Always allow students enough time to think about and to give their answers to the questions before clarifying the teaching.)

Ask students, What are some things that people are afraid of?

Is anyone afraid of bad people hurting them?

Is anyone afraid of God?

Jesus told His disciples to go tell other people about Him. Why did Jesus want His disciples to tell other people about Him?

Jesus wanted His disciples to go tell other people about Him so that other people could believe in Him and go to Heaven when they die.

But it was dangerous talking about Jesus back then. It was against the law and you could get arrested or even killed because of it.

(Have students take turns reading Matthew 10:16-18, or read it yourself.)

Jesus said that His disciples would be arrested and beaten if they go try to tell people about Jesus. That's because most people didn't want to believe Jesus. They just wanted to keep believing in God the wrong way or they wanted to believe in fake gods instead.

But Jesus told the disciples that when they get arrested and people start asking them questions, they shouldn't worry about it.

(Have students take turns reading Matthew 10:19-20, or read it yourself.)

Why shouldn't the disciples worry about what to say? (Because the Holy Spirit would give them the words to say.)

When we're talking to someone about Jesus, or someone is asking questions about what we believe, we don't have to worry about what we're going to say. We can trust God to give us good ideas about what to say. Jesus says that the Holy Spirit will make us think of the right things.

(Have another student read Matthew 10:21, or read it yourself.)

Jesus told the disciples that sometimes their family members wouldn't believe in Jesus and would get them in trouble because they did believe in Jesus. It's like that with us too. Maybe someone in your family, like your parents or grandparents, don't believe in Jesus or come to church. If your parents don't believe in Jesus, does that mean you can't believe in Jesus? (No.)

Jesus says that you should believe in God and Jesus even if the other people in your family don't believe in Him.

(Have students take turns reading Matthew 10:22-23, or read it yourself.)

Jesus told His disciples that if the people in one town don't want to hear about Jesus, they should go to another town. It's the same way with us. If we try to tell someone about Jesus and they don't want to hear about Him, does that mean we can't tell anyone else about Jesus? (No.)

If we try to tell someone about Jesus and they don't want to believe in Him, then we just have to try to tell someone else and maybe that person will believe in Jesus.

But even though Jesus said that the disciples would get in trouble for telling people about Him, He also told them not to afraid of people hurting or killing them.

(Have another student read Matthew 10:28, or read it yourself.)

Jesus says that we shouldn't be afraid of people who can kill us, but who should we afraid of? (God.)

If we believe in God and someone kills us, that would be sad, but it's okay because we know we'll go to Heaven.

But if we don't believe in God and we die, what will happen? (We'll go to Hell.)

So Jesus says to be more afraid of God than people, because people can only kill us, but God can send us to Hell if we don't believe in Him. If we do believe in Him, then He won't send us to Hell.

So remember, if someone in your family doesn't believe in Jesus, you can still believe in Jesus. And if you're telling someone about Jesus, trust God to help you know what to say. Be brave when you talk to people and He will help you.

Lesson 10: Wisdom is Proved Right by Her Actions

Needed: Bibles, pictures of various types of people

Lesson: (Note: Always allow students enough time to think about and to give their answers to the questions before clarifying the teaching.)

Show students pictures of various types of people. Make sure you're showing a variety of types of people (men, women, long hair, short hair, different races, different cultures, different countries, different styles of dress, including "Goth"). Show each picture to your students and ask, Is this person a good person or a bad person?

(Have a student read Matthew 11:18-19, or read it yourself.)

Some people thought that John was a bad person because he dressed in rags and ate bugs and lived in the desert and didn't like to eat nice food with people. Jesus did like to eat and drink with people, but some people still thought He was a bad person.

But Jesus says that wisdom is proved right by her actions. That means you can't decide if a person is good or bad just by looking at how they dress or what hairstyle they have or what color they are or where they're from or anything like that. You have to decide if they're a good person or not by what they do. Are they doing the right things that God wants them to do, or are they doing the wrong things that God doesn't' want them to do?

What people do is the only thing that matters to God, and if we believe in God, then that should be the only thing that matters to us too.

Lesson 11: Come to Me, All You Who are Weary and Burdened

Needed: Bibles, a heavy object (such as bricks or boxes of rocks)

Lesson: (Note: Always allow students enough time to think about and to give their answers to the questions before clarifying the teaching.)

Give students your heavy object. You can have an object for each of them or have them take turns holding one thing.

Say, Let's see who can hold this the longest. Whoever can hold it the longest, wins.

Was that pretty heavy?

Now try this. (Hand them each a Bible.) Is that a little less heavy?

(Have students take turns reading Matthew 11:28-30, or read it yourself.)

What does Jesus say He will do for those who are weary and burdened? (He will give them rest.)

What does it mean to be weary? (To be tired.)

What does it mean to be burdened? (To be carrying something heavy.)

Sometimes the heavy things we carry are sins. When we've done something wrong, it makes us feel guilty and when we feel guilty, it makes our souls feel heavy and sad.

Sometimes the heavy things we carry are worries. We worry about things and that makes our souls feel heavy.

But Jesus says He will take our heavy things and give us something lighter. We can give Him our sins and our guilt and He will forgive us. We can give Him our worries and then not worry about them anymore.

Then, when we give Jesus our sins and our worries, He gives us His rules to follow. But following Jesus' rules is much easier than making our souls by carrying around all those sins and worries. We can give Jesus our sins and the things we're worried about and all we have to do is follow His rules.

Lesson 12: Jesus Steals Us Back!

Needed: Bibles

Lesson: (Note: Always allow students enough time to think about and to give their answers to the questions before clarifying the teaching.)

Have a student read Matthew 12:29, or read it yourself.

Tell students, I want you all to close your eyes and imagine the story I'm about to tell you. There is a man, sitting in his house late at night. He has lots of nice things in his house and sitting in his chair, looking at all of them. But then, all of a sudden, a very strong man, much stronger than the man in the house, breaks through the door. The strong man fights with the man and beats him. He ties him up in the chair and then the strong man takes all of the man's nice things.

You can open your eyes for a second. Who do you think the good guy was in that story, the man who was sitting in his house, or the strong man who came in, tied up the other man, and then took all of his things?

Usually, we would say that the man in his house was the good guy and the strong man who tied up the man and took his things was the bad guy.

But now close your eyes and listen to the story again.

There is a man, sitting in his house late at night. The man is Satan, or the devil, and his house is the whole world. He has lots of nice things in his house and he's sitting in his chair, looking at all of them. The nice things that he has, though, is people. He's kidnapped all of the people from God by making them do bad things and turn against God. But then, all of a sudden, a very strong man, much stronger than the man in the house, breaks through the door. The strong man is Jesus. Jesus fights with the devil and beats him. He ties him up in the chair and then the strong man, Jesus, saves all of the people that the devil had kidnapped, and brings them back to God.

Now who is the good guy, the strong man, Jesus, or the man in the house, the devil?

Jesus is the good guy because He beats the devil and saves us all from him. Remember that Jesus is always stronger than Satan, and Jesus can always save us from him.

Lesson 13: If You're Not With Me, You're Against Me

Needed: Bibles (optional: something to represent two professional sports teams, such as pictures of their logo, jerseys, or hats)

Lesson: (Note: Always allow students enough time to think about and to give their answers to the questions before clarifying the teaching.)

Show students your two items. I'm using the Cowboys and the Bengals football teams for this example.

Say, Let's pretend you're going to be a pro football player and you want to join the Cowboys team. If you join the Cowboys team, can you also join the Bengals team and be on both teams at the same time? (No.)

What if you don't join the Cowboys team or the Bengals team. Let's say you change your mind and don't want to be on any football team. Are you on the Cowboys team then? (No.)

You have to actually be on the Cowboys team to be on the Cowboys team, right?

That's kind of the same way it is with Jesus and being a Christian.

(Have a student read Matthew 12:30, or read it yourself.)

Jesus said if you're not with Him, you're against Him. If you're not on His team, then you're on the devil's team. If you're on Jesus' team, if you believe in Jesus, then you'll go to Heaven when you die. But if you don't believe in Him, like maybe you believe in another religion, or maybe you don't believe in anything at all, then that means you're not on Jesus' team and you can't go to Heaven when you die. You have to be on Jesus' team, you have to believe in Jesus, if you want to go to Heaven.

And Jesus wants all of us to be on His team so that we can all go to Heaven when we die.

Raise your hand if you believe in Jesus and want to be on His team.

Lesson 14: Being a Part of Jesus' Family

Needed: Bibles (optional: pictures of people and the things they invented)

Lesson: (Note: Always allow students enough time to think about and to give their answers to the questions before clarifying the teaching.)

Show students a picture of the first car and ask, Who invented the world's first car? (Reveal the answer and then do the same for the first video game and the first cell phone.)

(Show the picture of the family.) Who invented the idea of the family? Whose idea was it for there to be moms and dads and kids and brothers and sisters? (God.)

God invented the family. God invented the family so that our parents could love and take care of us and so that we could learn from and be friends with our brothers and sisters. God likes us all to be in families that love and help us.

But as much as God likes our families, our families are not the only family that we have.

(Have students take turns reading Matthew 12:46-50, or read it yourself.)

Who did Jesus say His family is? (Those who do God's will.)

That means that if you believe in God and do the things God tells us to do, you are a part of Jesus' family. And if you believe in Jesus and I believe in Jesus, then that means we're family together because we're all part of Jesus' family.

And Jesus says that being a part of His family – believing in God and doing what God wants us to do – is even more important than the families that we live with, like our parents and brothers and sisters. Because believing in God and doing what God wants us to do is the most important thing there is.

Lesson 15: Saved by Faith

Needed: Bibles, drawing paper, crayons or markers

Lesson: (Note: Always allow students enough time to think about and to give their answers to the questions before clarifying the teaching.)

Tell students, I want you to close your eyes and imagine that a man killed another man and then went to jail. He was about to be put to death for murdering someone, but then the governor called the jail and told the jail not to kill the man, but to let him go free instead. How do you think that would make the man feel? (Good.)

Now I want you to think of one wrong thing that you have done. It could be not listening to your parents, or fighting with one of your friends at school, or calling someone a name. But then you said you were sorry about it and the other person forgave you. How does it feel when you know that someone else has forgiven you for the wrong thing that you did? (It feels good.)

Well, today, we're going to read a story about a woman who needed God to forgive her for some things that she had done wrong.

(Have students take turns reading Luke 7:36-37, or read it yourself.)

What kind of woman came to see Jesus? (A sinful woman, a woman who had done a lot of bad things.)

(Have students take turns reading Luke 7:38-39, or read it yourself.)

Did the Pharisee think that Jesus should let the woman touch Him? (No.)

The Pharisee thought that Jesus shouldn't let the woman touch Him because she had done too many bad things.

Why do you think Jesus let the woman touch Him?

I think it's because still Jesus loved her, no matter what bad things she had done.

(Have students take turns reading Luke 7:40-48, or read it yourself.)

What did Jesus say to the woman about all of her sins? (Jesus said that He forgave her for all her sins.)

Do you think Jesus can forgive you for all of your sins too? (Yes. Jesus can forgive us for anything that we have done.)

(Have students take turns reading Luke 7:49-50, or read it yourself.)

What did Jesus say saved the woman? (Her faith.)

Because she had faith in Jesus, her sins were forgiven and now she is saved. She won't have to go to Hell when she dies, but will go to Heaven. What do you have to do for your sins to be forgiven and to be saved? (Have faith in Jesus.)

It's as easy as that. If you believe in Jesus and believe that Jesus died on the cross to take the punishment for your sins, then God forgives you for all of your sins!

Craft: *Paired Portrait* – Have students draw a picture of themselves and the woman who was forgiven in the story together, both being happy that Jesus has forgiven them. Explain that Jesus has forgiven them just like He forgave the woman in the story.

Lesson 16: Growing in God – The Parable of the Sower

Needed: Bibles, seeds, dirt, (optional – planting pots for each student)

Lesson: (Note: Always allow students enough time to think about and to give their answers to the questions before clarifying the teaching.)

Before starting, go outside and clear a small patch of ground from grass, or bring in planting pots for each student.

Take children outside. Give them each a handful of seeds.

Tell students, Jesus told a story once about planting seeds. When we plant seeds, we want them to grow into plants, but sometimes seeds don't grow.

Let's take our seeds over to the sidewalk. Everyone put a couple of seeds down on the sidewalk…Good. Now, do you think those seeds will grow on the sidewalk? (No.)

What could happen to those seeds to make them not grow on the sidewalk?

People could step on them and ruin them. Birds or other animals could come up eat them. Also, there's no dirt on the sidewalk for the seeds to grow in.

Well, then let's take our seeds down the sidewalk a little bit and here, I'll pour a little dirt on the sidewalk over here (pour a thin layer). Now everyone put a couple of your seeds in the dirt...Good. Now do you think our seeds will grow?

They might grow a little bit, but there's still not very much dirt so our seeds won't be able to make strong roots that go very far down into the ground. I don't think our seeds will do very good here.

Let's go somewhere else. (Take students to the base of a tree or to some bushes.) What would happen if we put our seeds here? Would our seeds grow very well?

I think our seeds wouldn't grow very well because there are already some plants here.

What if we went over here? (Take students to cleared area or to your planting pots.) What if we planted our seeds here? Then would they grow?

Yes, they would grow because they have a lot of good dirt here and there's nothing else around to bother them.

Jesus said that our seeds are kind of like the truth about God. Lots of people hear about God, but not everyone believes in Him. Do you remember how we planted some seeds on the sidewalk without any dirt, and we said that birds or other animals could come eat them and take them away? Jesus said that sometimes when people hear the truth about God, the devil comes and makes them not want to pay attention to God, just like birds that steal the seeds away.

Then we tried to plant seeds on the sidewalk with just a little bit of dirt. We knew that wouldn't work because the seeds have to grow roots that go far down into the ground if we want them to be healthy. Jesus said that's like people who believe in God, but never go to church or try to learn anything more about God. They don't have good roots so they don't believe in God for very long.

Then we tried to plant our seeds where there was already something growing. Our seeds wouldn't do very well there because that spot was too busy already. Jesus said that would be like trying to believe in God, but never making any time for Him, like you're too busy for God.

But now we found a spot where we can plant our seeds and they will do well. Everyone plant your seeds in the dirt here.

Jesus said that if you want to be like good dirt and have the seed of God's truth grow in your lives, then you have to make sure that the devil doesn't make you forget about God, and you have to make sure that you're spending time with God and learning more about Him so that God's truth can make good roots in your life.

What are some things we can do to spend time with God and learn more about Him? (Read your Bible, pray, go to church, etc.)

And Jesus said that if you will do those things and let God's truth grow in your life, then you can start telling other people about God's truth and maybe they will start to let God's truth grow in their lives because you told them. It's like when a seed grows up into a plant, it makes more seeds. When you learn about God, it's like you're growing up to be a big plant for God and you

can give your seeds, what you know about God, to
other people so that they can learn too.

Lesson 17: The Good and Bad Seed – The Parable of the Weeds

Needed: Bibles

Lesson: (Note: Always allow students enough time to think about and to give their answers to the questions before clarifying the teaching.)

Tell students, I want you to close your eyes and imagine this story. A farmer went out and worked hard all day, planting seeds in his field. But then, while he was sleeping that night, his enemy came and secretly planted weed seeds in the farmer's field. When the plants started to grow, the farmer saw that some of the plants were the good seeds he had planted and some of them were weeds!

The farmer's workers asked the farmer, "Do you want us to go pull up all the weeds in the field?"

"No," the farmer said, "because while you're pulling up the weeds, you might accidentally pull up some of the good plants too. We'll let the good plants and the weeds grow together until it's time to cut the good plants down and put them in the barn. Then we'll pick the weeds out and burn them."

Okay. You can open your eyes. How did the farmer get weeds in his field? (An enemy planted them.)

The farmer is Jesus in this story, and He plants good seeds. His farm field is the whole world and the seeds He plants are people who believe in God and do the right things that God wants them to do. So the good plants are good people who believe in God.

Who do you think Jesus' enemy is? (The devil.)

The weeds the devil plants are bad people who do the wrong things that God doesn't want them to do. What does Jesus say will happen to the weeds in the end? (They will be burned up.)

And the Bible tells us that when people are bad and don't believe in God, then they will go to Hell when they die. That's sad because God doesn't want anyone to go to Hell, but some people will. We just have to make sure we believe in God and tell as many other people as we can to believe in God so that they can believe in God too and not go to Hell when they die.

What will happen to the good plants in the end? (They will be put in the barn.)

That's like Jesus taking all of the good people who believe in God and putting them in Heaven.

Lesson 18: A Little Bit Goes a Long Way – The Parables of the Mustard Seed and the Yeast

Needed: Bibles, seed, picture of a tree, bread without yeast, yeast, bread with yeast

Lesson: (Note: Always allow students enough time to think about and to give their answers to the questions before clarifying the teaching.)

Ask students, Do any of you know of any famous singers or music groups?

Who are they?

Did you know that at one time, those people were not famous? Maybe only a few people liked them, but since they were really good and their songs were really good, more and people heard about them and they got more and more popular. Their songs got played on the radio and they got to make CDs and music videos and play big concerts.

That's kind of how it is with Jesus.

(Have students take turns reading Matthew 13:31-33, or read it yourself.)

(Show students your seed.) Jesus said that the message about God started small, like this seed, because Jesus could only tell the people in His own country about God. But then, after Jesus died, His disciples went and told more and more people about God. They even went to other countries to tell people about God. And people are still doing that today. Christians go to other countries and tell people about God, just like you can tell your friends and family about God. More and people did believe and will still believe in God and that makes the message about God more popular. It's like the seed growing up to be a big tree. (Show picture of tree.)

The message about God is also like baking bread. (Give students a piece of unleavened bread.) What's wrong with this bread? (It's not tall, it's flat, etc.)

(Show students yeast.) This is what you put into bread to make it get taller. It's called yeast and you only need a little bit. If you use just a little bit of yeast, your whole loaf of bread will rise up. (Give students a piece of leavened bread.)

(Have students take turns reading Matthew 13:31-33, or read it yourself.)

The message about God started small, just like the small amount of yeast you need to bake bread, because Jesus could only tell the people in His own country about God. But then, as His disciples told more and more people about God, and as we tell more and people about God, then the message about God will get more popular, just like the little bit of yeast makes the whole loaf of bread rise up.

What is one thing you can do to help tell other people the message about God? (Tell your friends what you know about God, invite them to church or special church activities, etc.)

Lesson 19: Worth More than Anything – The Parables of the Hidden Treasure and the Pearl

Needed: Bibles, picture of a treasure chest

Lesson: (Note: Always allow students enough time to think about and to give their answers to the questions before clarifying the teaching.)

Ask students, What is the most important thing in the whole world? (Simply listen to their answers.)

What do you think God thinks is the most important thing in the whole world? (Again, just listen.)

(Have a student read Matthew 13:44.)

What did Jesus say the Kingdom of Heaven was like? (A treasure.)

And when the man found the treasure, what did he do? (He sold everything he had so he could buy the field and get the treasure.)

(Have students take turns reading Matthew 13:45-46.)

What else did Jesus say the Kingdom of Heaven is like? (A really expensive pearl.)

When man found the pearl, what did he do? (He sold everything he had so he could buy the pearl.)

So Jesus says that the Kingdom of Heaven is like a treasure or a really expensive pearl, and that when people found the treasure and the pearl, they gave up everything they had so they could get it. Getting the treasure or the pearl was the most important thing to them in the whole world. That shows us that getting into the Kingdom of Heaven should be the most important thing to us.

Getting into Heaven is worth everything. It's the most important thing there is.

How do we make sure we're going to go to Heaven when we die?

If we believe in Jesus and do the good things that God wants us to do, then we will go to Heaven when we die.

Activity: *Treasure Hunt* – Hide a picture of a treasure chest in any room where students are allowed to go. Tell them to go look for the treasure. When they find it, remind them that the treasure we get is going to Heaven when we die. Let the student who found the treasure hide it so that the rest of the group can look for it again. Continue playing as long as time allows, making sure to let everyone have a chance to hide the treasure before letting someone hide it twice.

Lesson 20: The Good and Bad Fish – The Parable of the Net

Needed: Bibles, pictures of happy and angry fish, paper bag or kiddie pool

Intro Game: *Angel Fishing!* – Photo copy the Happy and Angry fish patterns and place them in a kiddie pool (without water) or in a paper bag. Have students take turns closing their eyes and reaching in to pick a fish. When they pull one out, they open their eyes and decide what to do with the fish. If it's a Happy fish that they caught, they get to keep it and get a point for that fish. If it's an Angry fish, they have to put it in a common discard pile. The student with the most Happy Fish at the end wins.

Lesson: (Note: Always allow students enough time to think about and to give their answers to the questions before clarifying the teaching.)

(Have students take turns reading Matthew 13:47-50, or read it yourself.)

Jesus told another story about fish. He said the fishermen kept the good fish and put them in baskets, but they threw the bad fish away. Jesus also said that the fish were like people. The good people are the people who believe in God and do the right things that God wants them to do. What will happen to the good people when they die? (They will go to Heaven.)

God will keep them in Heaven, just like the fishermen kept the good fish in his basket.

And the bad people are people who don't believe in God and who do the wrong things that God doesn't want them to do. What will happen to people when they die if they don't believe in God? (They will go to Hell.)

God will send those people to Hell, just like the fishermen threw the bad fish away.

That's sad because God doesn't want anyone to go to Hell, but some people will because they decide not to believe in God. We just have to make sure we believe in God and tell as many other people as we can to believe in God so that they can believe in God too and not go to Hell when they die.

Lesson 21: John the Baptist is Beheaded

Needed: Bibles

Lesson: (Note: Always allow students enough time to think about and to give their answers to the questions before clarifying the teaching.)

Ask students, Can anyone think of a time when one of your friends, or maybe a brother or sister, wanted you to do something wrong? (The teacher should share a story here as well, in order to encourage the students to share.)

Can anyone think of a time when you wanted to do something wrong to show off for your friends? (Again, the teacher should share as well.)

Well, today we're going to read about a man who did something very wrong because someone else wanted him to and because he wanted to show off to his friends.

(Have students take turns reading Matthew 14:3-4, or read it yourself.)

King Herod had arrested John the Baptist because John kept telling the king that the king shouldn't steal his brother's wife and marry her. It would be like if your uncle stole your mom away from your dad and married her. That's a wrong thing to do.

Do you think the king liked it when John told him he was doing something wrong? (No.)

The king didn't like it when John told he did something wrong, but John knew that he had to say what was right, even if the king put him in jail for it.

(Have students take turns reading Matthew 14:5-8, or read it yourself.)

So the wife's daughter, King Herod's niece, did a dance for him on his birthday. He liked the dance so much that he said he would give her anything she asked for. What did she say she wanted? (She wanted the king to cut off John the Baptist's head and give it to her.)

Why did she say she wanted that? (Because her mom, the king's wife told her to say it.)

The king's wife was doing something wrong too. She left her husband so she could go marry the king. John the Baptist said it was wrong for her to do that, so she wanted to kill him.

Do you think King Herod should cut off John the Baptist's head just because the girl asked him to? (No.)

(Have students take turns reading Matthew 14:9-11, or read it yourself.)

Why did King Herod agree to cut off John's head? (He made a promise that he would give the girl whatever she asked for and because he wanted to show off in front of the guests at his birthday party.)

Do you think God wanted King Herod to cut off John's head? (No.)

Sometimes our friends ask us to do things that are wrong, or we want to do things that are wrong just to show off for other people, but we have to remember that doing the right things that God wants us to do is more important than doing what other people say, or showing off for other people. The most important thing is what God wants us to do.

If your friends ever ask you to do something that's wrong, what can you say to them? (Suggestions: No, God wouldn't want me to do that, That's not a good thing to do, That could hurt someone's feelings, Suggest a better idea, etc.)

(Have students take turns reading Matthew 14:12-13, or read it yourself.)

When John's followers told Jesus what happened, what did Jesus do? (He went off by Himself.)

Why do you think He wanted to be by Himself? (Because He was sad that John died.)

Jesus is sad when bad things happen to people and they die. But one day, Jesus will bring John the Baptist and everyone else who believes in Him back to life and we will never die again.

Lesson 22: It's What Comes Out of Your Mouth

Needed: Bibles, rotten food, candy, dirt

Lesson: (Note: Always allow students enough time to think about and to give their answers to the questions before clarifying the teaching.)

Summarize Matthew 15:1-20 with the following object lesson and discussion:

Show students a piece of rotten food. Ask, Should anyone eat something like this? (No.)

What would happen if you ate it? (You would get sick.)

Would it make you a bad person if you ate it? (No, it would just be gross.)

(Show students a piece of candy and then drop it in the dirt.) Should I eat this dirty piece of candy? (No.)

It would be gross if I ate that, right? But would it make me a bad person if I ate it? (No.)

(Have students take turns reading Matthew 15:10-11, or read it yourself.)

Jesus said it's usually not a sin to eat something, because it's not what goes into your mouth that makes you a bad person, even if what you're eating is gross. It's what comes out of your mouth that might be a sin. Jesus says that the things that we say sometimes are not very good.

What types of things might we say that God wouldn't be happy with? (Lying, calling names, saying bad words, being rude to people, etc.)

Jesus says that when we say those bad things, we are sinning. So let's remember to always think about what we're about to say and before we say it, ask ourselves if God would like what we're about to say or not. If what we're about to say is bad, let's try really hard to think of something else to say instead, or else just not say anything.

Prayer: Pray that God would help you and the students remember to only say good things.

(Give students a piece of clean candy.)

28679573R00033

Made in the USA
Lexington, KY
31 December 2013